# The A to Z of Animal Poetry

By Rob Palmer

Illustrated by Mike Borromeo

Published by EXP Publishing
Norwich, Norfolk, Great Britain



Uses OpenDyslexic, available at http://dyslexicfonts.com and
created by Abelardo Gonzalez

# THANKS

Thank you to all those who contributed to this book, both knowingly and unknowingly. It took sixteen years to take this book from concept to creation, so that's a lot of people who had some involvement in pushing me to finally finish it. Once again, a big THANK YOU to you all.

# CONTENTS

# The Ant

The life of an ant
Isn't much fun,
Eating the leaves
That were grown in the sun.

Feeding the Queen
And moving her eggs,
Must be a strain
On their poor little legs.

Marching in lines,
Building a nest.
They never slow down
Or stop for a rest.

Then one day from May
To the end of July,
Some ants grow wings
And learn how to fly.

On the Queen's orders
They move somewhere new,
And get back to work,
Because that's what they do.

They work as a team,
Day after day.
That's an ant's life,
What more can I say?

# Big Brown Bear

Big brown bear,
Sitting in a chair.
There's something wrong with that,
He's stroking my pet cat.

Big brown bear,
Wearing underwear.
That's not right at all,
They must be far too small.

Big brown bear,
Climbing up the stairs.
"Come down here you beast,
I'll cook you a big feast!"

Big brown bear,
The only one there.
He's put us in his belly,
And now he's watching telly.

# My Cat

Curling up upon the mat,
By the fire is where he sat,
Purring as he feels me pat,
Dreaming about catching a rat.

He likes to sit in my Dad's hat,
Playing with my Halloween bat.
I must admit, he's rather fat.
But I don't care, because he's my cat.

DEREK

# Derek the Dane

Derek the Dane was a dog,
Who used to think he was a frog.
He'd hop around and chase the flies,
But never caught one, though he'd try.

Because he was so very big,
Even larger than a pig,
He used to break all things in sight
And in the dark he was a fright.

He'd leap up, land on my bed,
Only just missing my head,
Then he'd walk to the bottom to sleep,
But luckily not on my feet.

He snored loud but never did bark
And made me feel safe in the dark.
No monster would dare make a sound
When Derek the Dane was around.

## Elephants

You may have already heard
About the elephants on parade.
But do you know of the travelling circus
With the elephants doing ballet?

With a long nose attached to their face,
They can balance and move with grace.
Leaping around the ring,
For their size, is a marvellous thing.

They can spin very fast round and round
And do the splits right down to the ground,
Then jump very high in the air,
In their tutus and pink underwear.

You'll never see something more elegant
Than this incredible herd of elephants.

# Filbert and Felicty

Jump jump croak,
Filbert catches flies,
From lilypad to lilypad,
Leaping through the sky.

Felicity is a flying frog,
She glides from tree to tree,
Eating jungle insects,
Her favourite way to be.

Although they are quite different,
One thing is the same.
They both compete at high jump
At the World Amphibian Games.

They leap and fly and fly and leap
Much higher than the rest,
So Filbert or Felicity
Will end up as the best.

Before they make their final jumps
They catch each other's eyes
And fall in love, as quick as that,
Then decide to share the prize.

Filbert and Felicity
Are high jump champions,
With lots of little tadpoles,
Their daughters and their sons.

# Guinea Pigs

I had two guinea pigs,
A girl and a boy.
One called Rosie,
One called Roy.

I'd clean their cage
Twice a week,
Change their water
And leave them treats.

Last time I took them
Out to play,
Rosie looked bigger
Than the previous day.

And then one morning
I heard lots of noise.
There were four more guinea pigs,
One girl, three boys.

I now have
Six guinea pigs to feed,
To clean their cage
And leave them treats.

The only problem,
And it's not funny,
Their food costs
All my pocket money.

# Hammy

I got a hamster for Christmas,
I called it 'Hammy' of course
And though I loved it so very much,
I really wanted a horse.

But a few months later,
On my tenth Birthday,
I woke with a yawn, early that morn,
To find 'Hammy' had run away!

I checked under the table,
I checked under my bed,
Mum even checked her ironing pile,
"Hammy's not there" she said.

Dad then stood up proudly
To tell us all his secret.
He'd given 'Hammy' to the school
And bought me a brand new pet.

I was led into the garden,
And introduced to Tony.
With a mouthful of Mum's best daffodils,
Yay! He was a pony!

# Iguanas

Lazy iguana wearing pyjamas,
Eating bananas topped with sultanas.

Active iguana wears a suit of armour,
Fighting the farmer to win some bananas.

# Jiggle Jiggle Jellyfish

Jiggle jiggle jellyfish,
Dancing through the sea.
Quickstepping, foxtrotting,
Jiving, diving.

Jiggle jiggle jellyfish,
A funny sight to see.
Like a jolly brolly
With strings that sting.

Jiggle jiggle jellyfish,
Floating for some food.
With a cha cha cha, salsa,
Rhumba, samba.

Jiggle jiggle jellyfish,
Brings a happy mood.
With boogie woogie grooves
And flippy floppy moves.

# Kudu

Curly horned kudu,
Chewing on the grass,
Wary of the predators,
Ready to run fast.

Cruising the savanna,
Looking for a friend,
Another wary kudu
To play with and defend.

Two curly horned Kudus,
Chewing on the grass,
Happy with their friendship,
Knowing it will last.

## Lotty

There once was a llama called Lotty,
That everyone thought was dotty.
She made silly faces, wore bright red braces
And trousers that were purple and spotty.

# Monkeys

If you travel to the jungle
And look up in the trees,
Through the twisted branches,
Amongst the many leaves.
You might spot a curly tail
Or a pair of furry knees,
Or if you're really lucky,
A whole tribe of monkeys.

Some are big and cuddly.
Some are rather small.
Some have long and orange hair.
Some have none at all.
But what they have in common
With each other and with you,
Is that they're very cheeky
And mischief makers too.

CLASS

# Nathan the Newt

Here's a story about Nathan.
He was a little green newt.
He always did what he was told
And was so quiet they thought he was mute.

Nathan didn't have any friends
Because he was the smallest one.
Instead all the bigger newts called him names
And never let him have any fun.

As the years passed, they all got older
And Nathan started to change.
Like all the other newts, he grew a bit bigger
But something about Nathan was strange.

He grew much longer and stronger
And showed big white teeth when he'd smile.
Because, as it turns out, Nathan wasn't a newt
But a big, newt eating, crocodile.

## Hoo Am I?

I live in a hole, in a tree
In the dark, big eyes help me see.
I can turn my head all the way round.
When I fly, I don't make a sound.

I go to sleep right through the day
And at night I come out to play.
Some people think I'm very wise
And sometimes I'm quite large in size.

Do you know yet, what I am?
Do you need a helping hand?
Have a guess, give it a try.
Hoo Hoo Hoo, who am I?

MENU

## Panda

The panda lived in a zoo,
But he didn't like eating bamboo.
He preferred all the nosh
That was a little bit posh,
Like risotto and souffle too.

## The Quail

The quivering quail
Was scared of a snail
And wouldn't say boo to a mouse.

But one day he tried,
And to his surprise,
He quacked and blew over a house.

## Raymond

Raymond likes to run
On roads in the midday sun,
Around the trees and rocks,
Dodging cars and trucks.
Racing is his sport,
Uniformed in shorts.
None of his prey can beat him,
No doubt they'll end up eaten.
Each race he entered he won.
Raymond likes to run.

## Suzie 'T' Snake

Susie the slippery snake,
Sleeps soundly inside a sock.
Susie snoozes, she seldom loses
Some sleep before seven o'clock.

# Turkeys

In the United Kingdom, once a year
There is a time all turkeys fear.
It's the twenty fifth day of December,
But they start to worry in mid September.
So some of them will fly away
To a country called the U.S.A.
Although no turkeys will return,
Because they didn't read and learn
About a holiday called Thanksgiving,
That, for turkeys, is unforgiving.
As just like Christmas in the UK,
A roasted turkey is dish of the day.

## Sea Urchin

Are you a cactus or a spiky ball
With little legs that help you crawl?
You look like a hedgehog but live under the sea
And you seem to eat nothing but boring algae.

Do all the bigger sea creatures think you're a toy?
Do they use you for games that they all enjoy?
Or are your spines sharp enough to keep them away
And stop them from trying to use you to play?

Maybe you're living a secret existence
That sends you to space an incredible distance,
Orbiting planets and star constellations
In your faster than light speed sea urchin space station.

Avoiding black holes and quasars and such,
Is easy for you with all the buttons you touch.
A universal explorer is the story I'm preferring,
Rather than a run of the mill, standard sea urchin.

## Veronica

Circling high above the sands,
Looking for food and somewhere to land,
To feast on the meat that the lions left over,
But not this strange vulture, who'd rather eat clover.

Veronica is a vegetarian vulture you see.
She doesn't eat animals but leaves from a tree.
She bites into bushes and munches on grass.
There's no competition, so she doesn't eat fast.

You could be mistaken for thinking this bird
Just doesn't like meat, but it's really absurd
That the reason for this, and yes it's quite crazy,
Is that our good friend Veronica's lazy!

When all the other vultures scavenge about,
Veronica just doesn't want to go out
And fly round in circles for hours and hours,
Getting so tired with no scraps to devour.

With a rumbling tummy, so hungry is she,
Veronica continues to sit in her tree
And nibble on leaves that are ever so near,
Watching the lions chasing the deer.

## The Wolf

The wolf is such a fearsome creature,
If you take it to school
It will eat your teacher.
It will eat your Granny,
It will eat your Mum,
It will eat your Dad, but you're the one.
At night when you go off to bed
You'd better watch out
Or it will eat your head.

# Animal X

Animal X is tall and scary,
It's teeth are sharp and it's paws are hairy.
It wanders from house to house at night,
Looking for scared little children to bite.

His razor sharp claws and bright red eyes,
Could make even a grown man cry.
He's got pointed ears and a spiky tail
And often lets out a mighty wail.

There's only one thing to stop this beast
From making you his next midnight feast.
If you make him laugh and ruffle his hair,
He'll turn into a teddy bear.

So if you should see him near your bed,
Remember this poem that you have read.
Just stand up tall and shout "Oi, buster!"
Then tickle him with a feather duster.

# Yakety Yak

This is a warning,
So you'd better turn back
If you ever realise
You're approaching a yak.

A simple "Hello"
Will be your first and last word,
As yaks like to talk,
But not one, the whole herd.

It doesn't seem to matter
At all what they say.
Their mouths will keep moving
'Til the end of the day.

Only when darkness
Has sent them to sleep,
Can you make your escape
With a very fast creep.

So heed this short tale
And watch where you're walking,
Or you'll waste a day listening
To loads of yaks talking.

ZEBRA DONKEY
ZONKEY

# Zonkey

Everyone's heard of a zebra
And some people have ridden a donkey.
But not many know of this odd little
Four legged equine that zoos call a zonkey.

Some like to wear their coats stripy.
Some have hardly any at all.
Some are quite scruffy and dumpy.
Some are quite slender and tall.

Though they come in many colours and sizes,
You'll know what it is straight away.
And while some people call them a zebroid,
The word zonkey is more fun to say!

www.ingramcontent.com/pod-product-compliance
Lightning Source LLC
Chambersburg PA
CBHW041224050726
47599CB00001B/68

* 9 7 8 0 9 5 7 5 6 5 5 0 0 *